Mexican Folk Art

Coloring Book

Marty Noble

DOVER PUBLICATIONS, INC.
Mineola, New York

PUBLISHER'S NOTE

Produced by the common people of Mexico for daily use in their homes or for local celebrations of religious and secular events, Mexican folk art is renowned for its whimsy, originality and unaffected charm. For this varied collection of ready-to-color illustrations, artist Marty Noble has drawn on a broad cross-section of folk art from many regions of Mexico: Guerrero, Jalisco, Puebla, Guadalajara, Oaxaca and others. She has rendered images from textiles, furniture, gourds, cloth, pottery and other authentic sources, depicting stylized plants and animals, geometric elements, nature spirits, religious figures, and much more. Full-color illustrations on the covers suggest the potential for creative coloring of these delightful images.

Copyright

Copyright © 2003 by Dover Publications, Inc.
All rights reserved.

Bibliographical Note

Mexican Folk Art Coloring Book is a new work, first published by Dover Publications, Inc., in 2003.

DOVER *Pictorial Archive* SERIES

This book belongs to the Dover Pictorial Archive Series. You may use the designs and illustrations for graphics and crafts applications, free and without special permission, provided that you include no more than four in the same publication or project. (For permission for additional use, please write to Permissions Department, Dover Publications, Inc., 31 East 2nd Street, Mineola, N.Y. 11501.)

However, republication or reproduction of any illustration by any other graphic service, whether it be in a book or in any other design resource, is strictly prohibited.

International Standard Book Number: 0-486-42750-1

Manufactured in the United States of America
Dover Publications, Inc., 31 East 2nd Street, Mineola, N.Y. 11501

Center–painted decoration for a horn comb, from San Antonio de la Isla (state of Mexico).

Border–various majolica tiles found on churches, buildings and homes of Mexico.

Nineteenth-century decorated chest from Olinala (state of Guerrero).

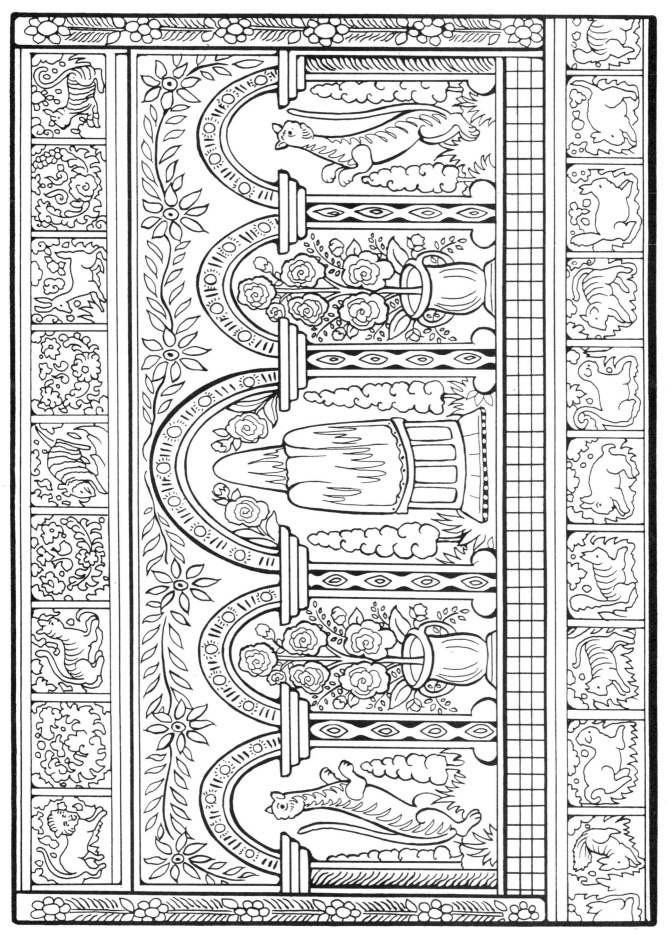

Design from painted chest—Olinala (Guerrero).

5

Center circular design—decoration from incised gourd rattle from the Mixtec village of Pinotepa de Don Luis, Oaxaca.

Border design—stylized Huichol floral pattern for sash.

6

Center image–decorative design for earthenware from Tonala (state of Jalisco).

Border design–diamond-within-diamond and hook motif from ceremonial cloth (Chontal).

7

Center image–decoration from incised gourd rattle from the Mixtec village of Pinotepa de Don Luis, Oaxaca. *Outer design–variants of diagonal bands with hook motif from woman's tunic (Mazatec).*

Center design—water bird design for earthenware from Tonala (Jalisco).

Outer design—vine motif composed of stepped squares and stylized floral elements from a woman's shoulder cape (Nahua).

Amate-paper painting of a horse, from Xalitla (Guerrero).

Star design found on textiles from the Otomi village of San Pablito, state of Puebla.

Center–skull design for a *popote,* a mosaic of little straws, from Mexico City.

Outer area–Mexican cut-paper design (*papel picado*) used during festivals.

Center design–from lacquerwork made with the technique of *rayado* in Olinala (Guerrero).

Border design–garland motif used for decorating walls, tiles and furniture.

Design for glazed petatillo ware of Tonala (Jalisco).

"Sacred Heart"–nineteenth-century Mexican cut-paper design (*papel picado*).

Yarn painting of a Huichol Indian ceremony.

16

Amate-paper painting of a village with cross from the village of Ameyaltepec (Guerrero).

18

Center design–from a paper cut made for the Festival of the Dead, Puebla.

Border design–detail from nineteenth-century cut-paper calligraphy.

Amate-paper painting from Guerrero.

Center design painted on tray (lacquerwork) from Olinala, Guerrero.

Center top design–from lacquered wooden tray, Urapan, Michoacan. *Center bottom design*–from juniper wood inlaid with abalone shell, Urapan, Michoacan.

Border–floral embroidery design from costume of southern Mexico.

21

Jaguars–detail from lacquered chest, Olinala, Guerrero.

Cut-out design (seed spirits) of bark paper from Otomi village of San Pablito, Puebla.

Detail of design from a *tibor* (ceramic jug), Guadalajara region, seventeenth century.

Amate-paper painting of lion and bird from Xalitla, Guerrero.

The Virgin of Guadalupe–cloth servilleta design from Otomi village, San Pablito, Puebla.

26

Design on polychrome-painted earthenware, Guadalajara region.

Embroidery design of plant and animal motifs, west central coast.

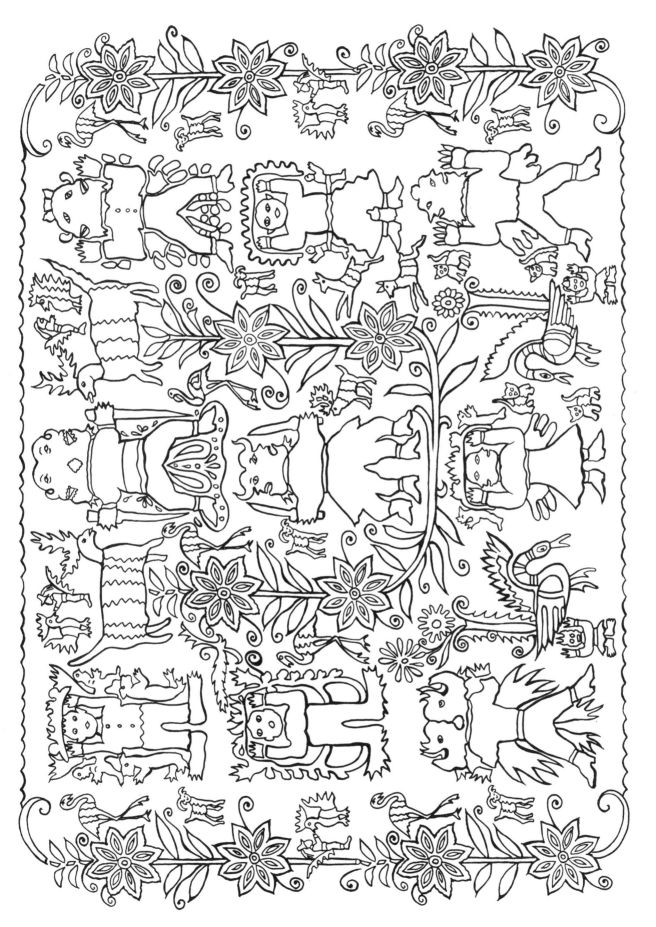

Otomi spirits—design on servilleta of factory cloth, San Pablito, Puebla.

Ceramic candlestick decorated with flowers and small figures, Metepec, state of Mexico.

Ceramic candlestick with religious figures, Metepec, state of Mexico.

Candelabrum of mermaids, sun, moon, stars, and fish, Acatlan, Puebla.